Brain Matters in Business

Brain Matters in Business

A COLLECTION OF ARTICLES ABOUT USING NEUROSCIENCE TO WORK SMARTER

JONATHAN JORDAN

Global Change Management, Inc.
Inspiring Business & Personal Development

Published by:
Global Change Management, Inc.
Inspiring Business & Personal Development

For additional copies of this book, please contact the publisher at +1 (321) 214-5824 or Info@MindfullyChange.com.

Book Editing & Design:
Cara Stein / BookCompletion.com

First Paperback Edition
ISBN-13: 978-0-9896616-0-7

Dedication

To Dad for influencing the development of my brain's left hemisphere; To Mum for influencing the development of my brain's right hemisphere.

Table of Contents

Introduction

Neuroscience research is producing an almost constant stream of new discoveries that are unlocking the secrets of how our brains work. For those of us directly involved in this research of the human brain, it is a very exciting time.

However, very few people outside of the neuroscience community understand these discoveries well enough to take advantage of them or apply them to their own lives in a way that gets meaningful results.

I see a need for simple, clear, accessible explanations of how to apply brain-based practices to greatly improve how we work and conduct business, so that everyone can benefit from these discoveries. A few years ago, I was invited to write a series of articles for publication, with exactly that goal. This book is a collection of those articles.

In addition to being supported by recent research of the human brain in the Western world, the articles in this book are also influenced by my knowledge of mindfulness and other ancient practices from the Eastern world. Interestingly, much of the recent neuroscience research confirms that many of these ancient Eastern practices do result in greatly improved brain functioning. The East-West synthesis evident in these articles reflects my many years of work and study on both sides of the Pacific Ocean, and my lifelong interest in how to improve the human brain.

If you would like to receive new articles in this series as they become available, simply send an email to Articles@MindfullyChange.com. Your email address will automatically be added to the notification list.

Keeping Your Brain in Mind:

How Neuroscience Improves Business Coaching Outcomes

New discoveries in neuroscience can help business coaches guide their clients to achieve better results, both in business and in their personal lives.

Using Functional Magnetic Resonance Imaging (fMRI), neuroscientists have discovered incredible new information about "neuroplasticity." Essentially, the term means an ability for new neural pathways to form in response to brain enrichment. A brain can change for the better at any age!

This discovery is probably the most astounding breakthrough in the history of neuroscience, ever.

The inaugural meeting of the NeuroLeadership Summit, founded by business coach David Rock, brought together business leaders, coaches, and neuroscientists to compare notes and plan ways to support one another. At that meeting, world-famous neuroscientist Dr. Jeffery Schwartz stated, "I see what coaching is now – it is a way of facilitating self-directed neuroplasticity."

Coaching has always been an exercise of the mind. With the more recent application of neuroscience breakthroughs, the coaching process has become even more effective at yielding positive results for our clients. Core activities of coaching, such as setting goals, making connections, becoming more aware, seeking breakthroughs, and taking action, parallel what neuroscientists tell us about how the brain operates. Coaches who keep the brain in mind typically are familiar with several models of change and collaborate with clients to match the model to the situation.

Business coaches who understand how the brain works can guide their clients in understanding that all success comes from their own minds.

Ultimately, the result is better outcomes for the clients. It stands to reason that coaching clients who have increased mental alertness and prolonged attention spans will do better than those who are mentally more sluggish.

Applying neuroscience-based business coaching models has been shown to improve the position of major corporations in terms of profitability, efficiency, and morale. When group members learn the focus of clear-minded critical thinking and communication, they can work with greater synergy as they strive toward the common goal of success. A coach who is knowledgeable of neuroscience-based practices can steer members of an organization onto a path that facilitates clearer thinking and sharper focus, which will benefit any organization, large or small.

Your Brain and Multitasking:

Why Multitasking Hinders Productivity And How To Fix It!

Do you believe you can multitask? Recent neuroscience research proves multitasking is a myth that can greatly hinder your productivity!

The human brain is a sequential processor, unable to consciously focus full attention on two tasks at the same time. Businesses praise multitasking and even create job descriptions that require employees to be able to multitask. However, research clearly shows that multitasking actually reduces productivity and increases mistakes.

Sure, we can do simple tasks like walking and

talking at the same time, but when it comes to true higher-level multitasking, your brain just can't do it. When you're walking and talking, you can't really pay attention to both tasks – this is why you will naturally pause your conversation as your feet negotiate steps or navigate around a pothole in the sidewalk. You need to pay attention to your walking so as not to fall over and hurt yourself. Your brain naturally focuses on conscious tasks sequentially.

So why do people swear they're more productive when they multitask? Like many beliefs about business functions, it is an illusion!

We have all seen the person working on his laptop with a cell phone awkwardly placed against his ear, loudly conversing with the person on the other end as his fingers peck away at an application on his laptop, which probably has several windows open. If challenged, he'd probably say, "I get more work done when I do several things at the same time." Does this sound like someone you know, maybe you sometimes?

Because "multitasking" drains a lot of mental and physical energy, we feel like we're productive. We worked hard and used energy, so we must have produced a lot, right? Wrong.

Another illusion is that multitasking saves time.

In fact, it consumes and wastes your time. What we call multitasking is really our brains attempting to switch our attention rapidly back and forth between tasks. But every time you switch your attention, your brain goes through a sequence of activities to refocus and adjust. If you attempt to focus on a task while still working on a previous task, your brain literally stalls for at least 300 milliseconds. These "processing gaps" might only take a fraction of a second, but when repeated many times per minute, the wasted time quickly adds up.

In addition, we lose track of previous progress and find ourselves needing to "start over," perhaps muttering things like, "Now where was I?" This results in not only a waste of time but also an increase in mistakes – both of which can damage your productivity.

In his book, *Brain Rules,* neuroscientist John Medina states that a person who is attempting to multitask takes up to 50 percent longer to accomplish a task, and he or she makes up to 50 percent more mistakes than a person working sequentially.

Cynthia Shapiro, a human resources expert and the author of *Corporate Confidential,* notes that even though corporations say they want employees who can multitask, what they really want is workers who have "laser focus on each and every task."

So if you shouldn't attempt to multitask, what should you do to increase productivity and accuracy?

- Organize and prioritize your tasks in advance. Create a daily task schedule first thing in the morning, or last thing in the evening before you leave the office the day before.

- Become familiar with your natural rhythms and know what time of the day you have the most energy – mental and physical. Schedule tasks accordingly.

- If possible, vary the sort of tasks you work on throughout the day. Your brain functions better when it has variety.

- Focus completely on one task at a time and complete it. Then focus on the next task. Keep repeating the process.

- Acknowledge the satisfaction you feel after the completion of each task, no matter how small the task. This will reinforce sequential task completion.

- Schedule times during the day when you will check your e-mail and voicemail – and be strict about only checking it during those designated times. This alone will greatly reduce multitasking temptations.

- When possible, turn off your e-mail notification, phone ringer, IM program, etc. – distractions that can waste your time and give you an illusion of being productive and important.

- Take "brain breaks" about once an hour. For example, stand up, stretch, and take a few slow deep breaths. Your brain will function better with movement and more oxygen.

Perform the above actions for at least a week. Then check to see whether you are more productive and accurate in your work than when you "multitasked" – you will be!

How Pricing Affects Your Brain

"We have known for a long time that people's perceptions are affected by marketing, but now we know that the brain itself is modulated by price," said Baba Shiv, a professor at the Stanford Graduate School of Business, in reference to a recent study. Although many studies have looked at how marketing affects behavior, this is the first to show that it has a direct effect on your brain.

In the study, while the subjects' brain activity was being monitored, they were given wine to taste. Some were told the wine was very expensive and some were told it was inexpensive – but it was exactly the same wine tasted by all. The monitored brain activity of the subjects who were told the wine was expensive showed significant increases in the part of the brain that registers pleasure: the medial orbitofrontal cortex. The subjects who were told the wine was inexpensive did not exhibit the same response.

This study shows that perceptions of quality trigger activity in the part of the brain that registers pleasure. Conversely, if a product or service is perceived as being of low value – even if it really is of high value – your brain will respond as if it was of low value.

Many business owners are tempted to discount their prices in order to increase sales. This study suggests that if discounting causes the product or service to be perceived as less valuable, it will have a negative impact on the prospects' brains, which will result in fewer sales, not more.

In addition, keep in mind that discounting damages your profit margin to a greater degree than the amount of the discount. For example, say your profit margin is 20 percent and you discount your price by 10 percent. You have actually reduced your profit margin by a huge 50 percent! (Discounts are usually applied to the gross price, not to the net profit, so a 10 percent discount shaves half off a 20 percent profit margin.)

What if, instead of discounting, you increased your prices by 10 percent? Would prospects consider your product or service to be more valuable? If so, their brains will respond positively, according to this study.

Sure, you might lose a few customers if you increase your prices, but remember, you can often greatly increase your profit margin by just a 10 percent increase in price. A 10 percent price increase would boost a 20 percent profit margin to 30 percent, which actually results in 50 percent increase in profit! So even if you did lose a few customers by increasing your prices, you could well end up with more net profit overall, due to the increased profit margin.

Additionally, your customers will experience more pleasure because they perceive an increase in value – and happy customers are usually repeat customers.

According to Professor Shiv, "Marketers are now going to think twice about reducing the price. If an experience is pleasurable, the brain will use it to help guide future choices."

I strongly encourage you to think twice before giving in to the temptation to discount your prices in an attempt to increase sales. Because of the way our brains respond to pricing, increasing your prices may well be a better way to increase your sales.

How to Calm Your Brain During Any Storm

There is a major storm in our economy today. Understandably, this situation results in many entrepreneurs feeling very stressed.

When you're overly stressed, the chemistry in your brain changes. Your problem-solving abilities are reduced, and your judgment is greatly diminished. In fact, it is a very similar state to being drunk!

This is no state to be in when making important decisions about your business or your life. As the markets hit tremendous lows in 2009, many investors panicked under the stress and sold all their investments. In most cases, this was a major mistake because they sold low and locked in all those losses. They did so because they were stressed and not thinking clearly.

Here are some simple steps you can take to begin to relax and reduce the effects of stress on your brain:

- Take at least 3 deep, slow, regular breaths. This will start to slow your heart rate, lower your blood pressure, and restore cognitive clarity.

- As you breathe, let your shoulders relax and loosen your jaw – you may be surprised at how much tension you hold in your jaw.

- Focus your mind on the present moment. To help with this, you might focus your attention on your breath passing through your nostrils as you breathe, or pick a spot on the wall and focus your eyes gently on that spot. When focusing on the present moment, you prevent yourself from regretting the past and fearing the future – both of which increase stress. (For a deeper understanding of this concept, read *The Power of Now* by Eckhart Tolle.)

- When uncomfortable feelings arise, don't try to ignore them. Instead, acknowledge and label them. Recent research at UCLA

> proves this technique allows you to detach from negative emotions and keep them from hijacking your calm.

You may also want to take a break. One good idea is to go for a walk in the fresh air and sunlight.

Once you sense you are relaxed, start to look at your situation more realistically. Then, like the serenity prayer says, accept the things you cannot change and have the courage to change the things you can.

Regarding the things you cannot change, simply accept the situation and let go of any tension you feel about it. If there is nothing you can do about it, why worry?

For the things you can change, use your state of calm and mental clarity to help you make an objective list of what you need to do – not one swayed by emotion. Then, in a calm and relaxed manner, complete each task to the best of your ability.

Will this calm the outer storm in our economy? No. But it will calm the storm within your brain and make you less likely to do something irrational that you will later regret.

Create Brain Trust and Rapidly Build Rapport

When your brain notices a person in the environment, it is programmed to decide quickly whether or not to treat that person as a threat. It takes less than 1/24th of a second for a human brain to react to this first impression at the unconscious level. Within three seconds, that first impression is firmly established and unlikely to undergo further significant change.

If the first impression someone has of you is perceived as threatening, any possibility of establishing meaningful rapport is lost. The threat does not have to be real, it only requires a *perception* of a threat – and when in doubt, the human brain tends to perceive a threat.

One expert in the field, Bruno Catellani of the Institute of Communication, Management and Sales in Switzerland, refers to this primitive brain function as the "gatekeeper." If your initial interaction with someone stresses that person's gatekeeper, it will switch on the fight-or-flight response (more clinically referred to as the activation of the brain's sympathetic nervous system). That includes shutting down message receptors and terminating any meaningful rapport with that person.

This neurological mechanism was necessary during our evolutionary development – in order to survive as a species, when our cave-dwelling ancestors saw a saber-toothed tiger, they needed to react with lightening speed.

Although we have mostly outgrown the need for such a rapid response to perceived threats, it is still hardwired in our brains, standing in the way of building rapport with others.

In short, when someone first becomes aware of you (in business or in any environment), you have less than three seconds to make a positive, nonthreatening impression.

How do you get past this neurological gatekeeper and build rapport with others? The opposite of a threat is trust – if you're trusted, you can't be a threat. Therefore, if you create the conditions for trust, you will prevent anyone from perceiving you as a threat, and you will be able to build rapport.

You need to establish yourself as trustworthy in those crucial first three seconds to make a first impression that gets past the brain's gatekeeper. Here are a few tips to help you rapidly create neurological trust and build rapport with anyone:

- First, smile. Nothing disarms a perceived threat as much as a smile. Even if your first contact is via the phone, smile – it will be reflected in your voice and overall attitude. (I have a mirror by my office phone so I can make sure I am smiling when I'm on the phone.)

- Use open, friendly, relaxed body language in your movements, gestures, facial expression, and eye contact. Reflect enthusiasm with your posture. Again, even when using the phone, your body language is subtly reflected in your voice and breathing. (I actually stand up and use a positive body posture for at least the initial part of a phone interaction.)

- Use a calm tone and voice modulation. Speak steadily, and don't talk too fast. By the way, as Professor Albert Mehrabian of

UCLA has documented, the actual words that you use are far less important than your body language, tone of voice, etc. The brain's gatekeeper decides whether or not to treat you as a threat before the brain can comprehend the meaning of your words.

- Choose your clothes and overall appearance to be appropriate for the situation. For example, if you run a childcare center, multiple facial piercings probably will not build trust with parents. However, if you run a tattoo parlor, maybe multiple piercings are appropriate.

- Smell good – or at least don't smell bad. Interestingly, olfactory inputs (smells) are processed by the brain more quickly than inputs from any other senses. Very often, it is an unconscious smell that first causes someone's brain to determine whether to treat you as a threat. By the way, guys, research shows most women perceive a man who uses too much cologne or aftershave as untrustworthy.

- Respect other people's personal space. Don't stand too close. At the same time, don't stand too far away – too much physical distance creates an emotional distance. However, when in doubt, give the other person space.

Once you have impressed on the brain of the other person that you can be trusted, you can easily and comfortably build a genuine rapport that will be beneficial to both of you.

The Social Brain and Workplace Teams

Most business leaders strive to improve their teams' performance. The study of the human brain, particularly in the area of social neuroscience, is providing some exciting insights that can help.

David Rock, the author of *Your Brain at Work,* discusses the importance of what he describes as "relatedness" in the workplace. He points out that "relatedness is a basic need of our social brain and is also a major driver of team behavior… 'safe social interactions' are essential for one to have a sense of relatedness in the workplace."

The work environment has an immense effect on people's attitudes, motivation, and performance. According to Rock, this concept of relatedness is closely linked to neurological trust. If our social brain does not have a strong sense of relatedness, we cannot fully trust.

The more people trust one another, the stronger the collaboration, the more information is shared, and the stronger the team. (See article 5 for more information about the brain and trust.)

In a work environment that lacks such relatedness, the brains of employees generate a threat response, which can greatly increase stress levels. Stress negatively impacts employees' neurological, physiological, and social functioning.

This can be detrimental to a business in many ways. Smart leaders know that the best way to keep their business strong and their employees motivated is to ensure that everyone has a sense of belonging and relatedness. By focusing on building the mindset of a trusting team, managers can improve not only employee morale but also productivity and the quality of work.

In order to foster a team mindset and ensure all employees are on the same page, a daily team meeting is highly recommended. Ideally, such a meeting addresses all issues in an inclusive manner that engages every employee, so they feel safe, trusted, and valued as team members, rather than feeling like isolated lone workers.

Business leaders who are worried about time

management may consider this practice to be a waste. However, the result is a more trusting team that works in harmony rather than discord, and the practice will actually save time and money in the long term. This assertion is supported by a Gallup report in November 2008 that showed organizations that encourage "water cooler" conversations increased productivity.

The pressures of the modern workplace can sometimes be too much to allow people to get to know each other during the average workday. Therefore, it is often helpful to occasionally organize team-building events and exercises away from the office.

Such activities do not need to be complicated or expensive, and they can be enjoyable for everyone involved. Activities like camping trips, golf, and boating can be great ways to enhance the team spirit and further develop a sense of relatedness.

A wise manager may even invite employees out for a drink or dinner after work. While this does not fall within the workday, it can definitely serve to bring team members closer together, strengthen that essential sense of relatedness, and further build trust.

Most business leaders today are faced with the

challenge of creating unified, high-performing teams from a host of diverse employees with different personality styles and a variety of cultural backgrounds. Anyone who manages people will benefit from understanding the basics of social neuroscience.

A Brain-Based Model for Effective Business Systems

The exit plan for all business owners should include creating a profitable venture that can operate without the owner. When a business reaches this stage, the owner has created an income-producing investment, rather than a self-employed job.

A business that does not rely on the owner to work in it greatly increases in value and gives the owner the luxury of either selling it for a nice profit or using the income stream to finance the owner's desired lifestyle and other activities. But how does an owner create a business that can operate without him or her? The answer is simple: develop and implement efficient systems.

Neuroscientist John Medina states in his book, *Brain Rules*, "Taking your sequential brain into a multitasking environment can be like trying to put your right foot into your left shoe."

Recent research clearly shows that attempting to multitask actually reduces productivity by up to 50 percent and increases mistakes by up to 50 percent. Therefore, businesses that mirror the brain's natural sequential processing of tasks have a strong competitive edge. (See article 2 for more information on multitasking.)

From my experiences as an executive with the McDonald's corporation and coaching hundreds of smaller businesses worldwide, I've designed six steps to creating effective business systems that work with – not against – the way your brain naturally functions:

1) **Start creating basic systems.** Chances are, you already have a systematic way of performing at least some of your business functions.

   You just haven't thought of them as "systems."

   If you have few or no systems in place, your business is probably in chaos. In that case, I highly recommend you start creating systems immediately so you decrease the chaos.

2) **Document your systems.** How do you commu-

nicate your systems to your team if they aren't recorded somewhere? Verbally explaining your systems over and over can be a huge waste of your valuable time.

Having well-documented systems actually increases the value of your business to a prospective buyer. When people purchase a franchise, a McDonald's restaurant for example, what they are really buying is a documented system that is proven to produce income. Document your systems "as if" you were developing a franchise manual, and not only will you increase the efficiency of your business, you will increase its value.

A quick tip: documentation means it is recorded in some medium. It's not limited to writing—you can also use videos to record how your systems work. Using videos instead of written documentation can save you a lot of writing, and videos may be more helpful when training others how to use your systems.

---

3) **Train your team on how to use your systems.** Don't assume that, because you created a system,

others will follow it. You need to have them trained in order for them to follow the systems you created. Systems documented on video often enhance the training process because about 30 percent of our brains are dedicated to processing visual input.

4) **Implement your systems.** Why go to the trouble of creating and documenting a system and training your team if you aren't going to implement the system? Unfortunately, I've discovered that many business systems are never fully implemented.

5) **Measure the results of your systems.** It's great to have systems, but unless you measure the results, how do you know if they're working well?

6) **Use the measurement results to improve your systems.** The Japanese have a concept they call "kaizen," which means continuously improving what you do. Even if your systems are working well, you can often tweak them for even better results.

The best way to train your brain and harness the power of neuroplasticity is to focus on a specific task and frequently repeat that task. (See article 1 for more information about neuroplasticity.)

The more you focus on and repeat a task, the easier it is for your brain to remember and complete the task. And the more you train your brain in this manner, the less energy your brain requires to complete those tasks. Creating systems not only helps your business, it helps your brain.

How to Use Your Whole Brain to Make Your Dreams Come True

Your brain has two hemispheres or sides: left and right. Typically, each hemisphere has different general abilities. For example, your ability to be creative, to dream, and to have a vision of the future is usually on the right side of your brain. Your ability to make and execute logical, practical plans is usually on the left side.

Many would-be entrepreneurs have a wonderful vision of the future but little or no plan of how to get there. They are right-brain dominant. On the other hand, many beginning entrepreneurs possess very practical or technical skills, but no real ability to see the larger picture. They are left-brain dominant.

Unfortunately, both groups have a high failure rate because they do not fully utilize the natural abilities in both sides of their brains.

Maximizing the potential of both hemispheres of our brain leads to greater success.

So how can you use the natural power of both sides of your brain, not just to dream, but also to make those dreams come true? Here are some tips for you:

- When creating your desired vision, stimulate the right side of your brain by putting logic aside for a while and allowing yourself to dream and be creative. Unleash the power of your imagination.
- Use as many senses as possible to record your vision. For example, write it down, draw it or create a vision board using pictures that represent what you want, and tell others about it. Each sense uses different areas of your brain, so the more senses you involve, the more of your brain power you'll use.

- Once you have created and recorded your vision, it is time to simulate the left side of your brain – the practical side. Think of the vision you created as the destination. Now, plan concrete and logical steps to reach that destination and make it a reality.

- Write your plan down. Place it and your vision board somewhere where you will see them frequently. Every time you see these things, it activates the areas of the brain you used to create them and brings your dream closer to reality.

Ned Herrmann, a neuroscientist and author of *The Whole Brain Business Book,* calls this sort of processing "whole brain functioning."

In order to understand whole brain functioning, think of how most people take a vacation. For example, a couple of years ago I saw an article in the *National Geographic* about the Grand Canyon, and I decided to go there on vacation. Once I decided where I was going, I planned how to get there. Finally, I executed the plan and was rewarded with a wonderful time in one of the most spectacular places in the world.

This trip started as a dream on the right side of my brain. It became a reality because I used the left side of my brain to plan and execute my dream.

When you go on a vacation, do you drive to the airport without knowing where you are going, enter the terminal, see where the various airlines are flying to that day, and then decide where to go?

That might be an interesting way to spend a vacation, but is it the best way to live your life or run your business? When it comes to your life and your business, are you drifting along, waiting to see where you end up, or do you have a destination in mind that you are actively moving toward? Do you have concrete plans on how to get there?

Instead of only using the dominant side of your brain, capture the natural power of both sides. You'll be wildly more successful.

Updates

If you would like to receive new articles in this series as they become available, simply send an email to Articles@MindfullyChange.com. Your email address will automatically be added to the notification list.

About the Author

Jonathan Jordan, a business & executive coach and member of the prestigious Society for Neuroscience, began his career in the Himalayan kingdom where the Buddha was born. Having learned the language and immersed himself in the culture there, he discovered ancient Eastern practices that increased his ability to train his brain and improve his life.

Jonathan, who grew up in Ireland, later became a licensed psychotherapist in the United States. In his practice, he successfully blended these Eastern practices with Western knowledge to greatly improve the wellbeing of his clients.

Jonathan has also successfully served as an executive for Fortune 500 Corporations, where he has led global initiatives to create cutting-edge brain-based training and development programs. These programs positively impact millions of employees worldwide every year.

Jonathan has been appointed a Faculty Fellow of Florida State University. Through nationwide and international seminars, he trains scores of other professionals and business leaders in his unique synthesis of East-West practices, which can greatly improve human performance at work and in all areas of life. In 2011, Jonathan was engaged by the United States Senate to deliver brain-based professional development workshops to the entire US Senate Staff on Capitol Hill in Washington, DC.

Jonathan is currently the president of a boutique business and personal development firm, Global Change Management, Inc. There, he utilizes mindfulness and other brain-based practices to guide clients to obtain greater success and satisfaction in their business, career, and life in general. For more information, please visit www.MindfullyChange.com.

Printed in Poland
by Amazon Fulfillment
Poland Sp. z o.o., Wrocław

76458183R00031